This book
belongs to

....

Counting Birds

Written and illustrated by Alice Melvin

Tate Publishing

For Will, who helped with the words, and a lot more besides.

The house sleeps still through the warm dark night,
but something stirs in the dawn's half-light…

Cock-A-Doodle-Doo!

One noisy cockerel is greeting the sun.
Another spring morning has barely begun.

1

Two lovebirds, nestled asleep in the hall,
are the first to be shaken awake by his call.

Three flying ducks, in a decorative row,
are suddenly bathed in the bright morning glow.

Four baby birds raise their beaks from the nest,
squawking and squealing their breakfast request.
But which is the cuckoo? Look – can you see?
(He's at least twice as big as the other three!)

5

Another young baby is sleeping in bed,
while five fabric birds gently turn overhead.

Hidden outside in the thick garden shrubs,
six small brown wrens are hunting for grubs.

Magpies in cherry trees chatter and scold.
'Seven for a secret never to be told!'

Pecking the ground is the mother hen's brood,
eight fluffy chicks are all searching for food.

Strutting about in the heat of midday,
nine handsome peacocks are out on display.
With beautiful feathers of turquoise and blue,
a great host of eyes seems to look straight at you!

9

The china's been laid out for afternoon tea.

Look – there are ten birds on the white crockery!

Eleven small chaffinches fly down to find
the raisins and crumbs that have been left behind.

11

Whirling above in the cloudless blue sky,
twelve racing pigeons go hurrying by.

12

Way down below, as the pigeons can see,
thirteen bright pheasants parade round a tree.

Fourteen white swans hold their heads up high,
their stately procession glides gracefully by.

14

15

Dipping and diving, with bottoms on show,
fifteen damp ducks bob their heads down below.

Waddling back to the yard in a crowd,
sixteen large geese honk and gabble out loud.

As day turns to dusk and the sun starts to set,
seventeen starlings are not asleep yet.
Up on the chimneys they noisily chat,
safe from the claws of the tortoiseshell cat.

Gathered on overhead wires nearby,
eighteen tired swallows are watching the sky.

18

Nineteen black rooks flock in tumbling flight,
returning to roost in the darkening night.

On red patterned curtains inside the bedroom,
twenty birds nestle to keep out the gloom.

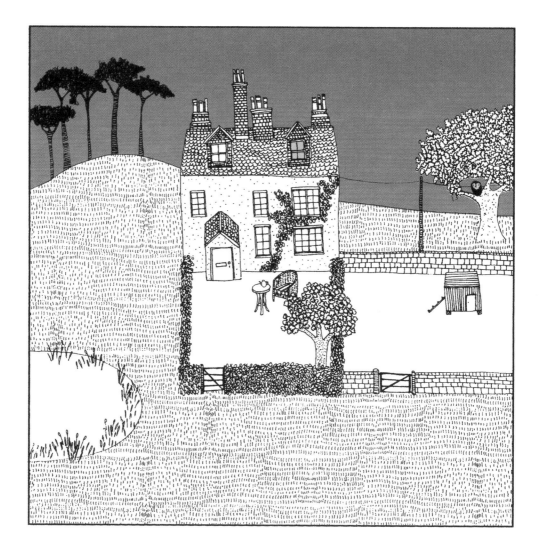

All are asleep now, so none of them see
the solitary barn owl awake in the tree.
With soft silent wings he slips into the night,
while the house waits once more for the dawn's half-light.

The End

First published 2009 by order of the Tate Trustees
by Tate Publishing, a division of Tate Enterprises Ltd,
Millbank, London SW1P 4RG
www.tate.org.uk/publishing

British Library Cataloguing in Publication Data
A catalogue record for this book is available from the British Library

ISBN 978 1 8543 7 8852

Distributed in the United States and Canada by Harry N. Abrams, Inc., New York

Library of Congress Cataloging in Publication Data
Library of Congress Control Number: 2009927427

Printed and bound in China by C&C Offset Printing Co. Ltd
Colour reproduction by DL Interactive Ltd, London

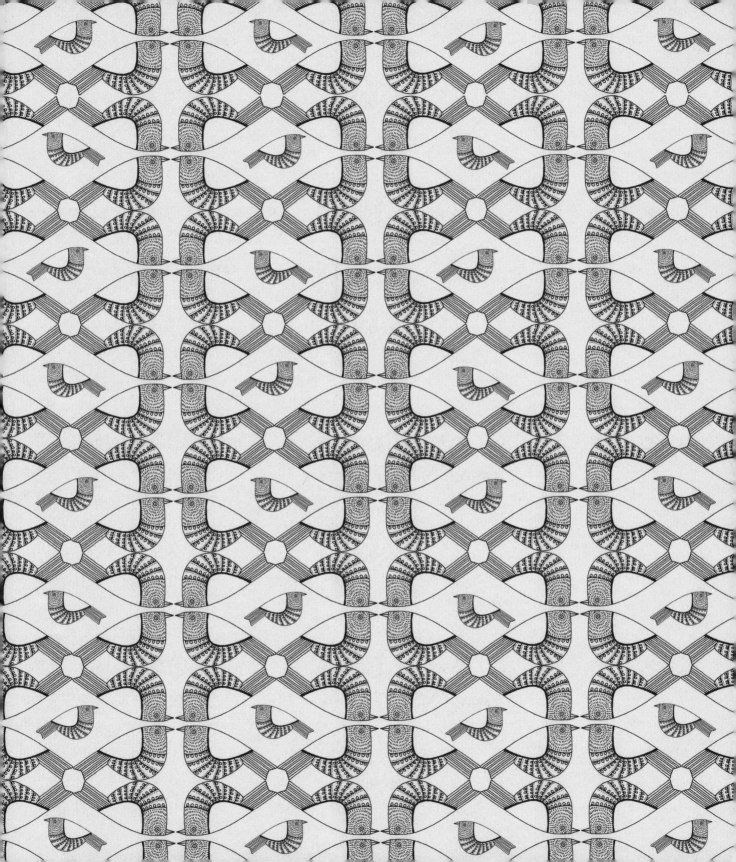